LEADING WOMEN

Kate Middleton

From Commoner to Duchess of Cambridge

KATE SHOUP

Cavendish Square
New York

Published in 2015 by Cavendish Square Publishing, LLC
243 5th Avenue, Suite 136, New York, NY 10016

Copyright © 2015 by Cavendish Square Publishing, LLC

First Edition

Website: cavendishsq.com

This publication represents the opinions and views of the author based on his or her personal experience, knowledge, and research. The information in this book serves as a general guide only. The author and publisher have used their best efforts in preparing this book and disclaim liability rising directly or indirectly from the use and application of this book.

CPSIA Compliance Information: Batch #WS14CSQ

All websites were available and accurate when this book was sent to press.

Library of Congress Cataloging-in-Publication Data
Shoup, Kate, 1972-
Kate Middleton : from commoner to Duchess of Cambridge / Kate Shoup.
pages cm. — (Leading women)
Includes bibliographical references and index.
ISBN 978-1-62712-981-7 (hardcover) ISBN 978-1-62712-983-1 (ebook)
1. Catherine, Duchess of Cambridge, 1982- 2. Princesses—Great Britain—Biography. 3. William, Prince, Duke of Cambridge, 1982- -Relations with women. I. Title.

DA591.A45W5577 2014
941.085092—dc23
[B]
2014002020

Editorial Director: Dean Miller
Editor: Andrew Coddington
Copy Editor: Cynthia Roby
Art Director: Jeffrey Talbot
Designer: Amy Greenan/Joseph Macri
Photo Researcher: J8 Media
Production Manager: Jennifer Ryder-Talbot
Production Editor: David McNamara

The photographs in this book are used by permission and through the courtesy of: Cover photo, 1, Chris Jackson/Getty Images; Peter Macdiarmid/Getty Images, 4; Splash News/Newscom, 9; © David Parker/Solo/ZUMAPRESS.com, 15; Tim Graham/Tim Graham Photo Library/Getty Images, 18; AP Photo/Jeff J. Mitchell, Pool, 24; © Malcolm Clark/Solo/ZUMAPRESS.com, 28; Max Mumby/Indigo/ Getty Images, 30; Michael Dunlea/AFP/Getty Images, 31; Anwar Hussein/Getty Images, 32; Anwar Hussein Collection/ROTA/FilmMagic/Getty Images, 37; AP Photo/Kirsty Wigglesworth, 38; © Solo/ ZUMAPRESS.com, 42; © AP Images, 44; Photoshot/Newscom, 46; Anwar Hussein/Getty Images, 50; Samir Hussein/WireImage/Getty Images, 52–53; AP Photos/APTN, 55; © AP Photo/Matt Dunham, 57; Chris Ison/PA Wire URN:10620265 (Press Association via AP Images), 58; Rex Features via AP Images, 60; Allpix/Splash News/Newscom,65; Press Association via AP Images, 67; WPA Pool/Getty Images, 68; Rex Features via AP Images, 71; Oli Scarff/Getty Images, 72; Max Mumby/Indigo/Getty Images, 74; Rex Features via AP Images, 81; JOHN STILLWELL/AFP/Getty Images, 82; JASON BELL/EPA/Newscom, 84.

Printed in the United States of America

CONTENTS

CHAPTER ONE

Berkshire Beginnings

April 29, 2011 was a day to remember. As an estimated two billion people worldwide watched on television, Miss Catherine "Kate" Middleton made history. Dressed in a stunning white Alexander McQueen gown, Middleton exchanged wedding vows with Prince William Arthur Philip Louis.

It was a grand occasion. Experts estimate that the event cost some $32 million (£20 million). However the wedding, which took place in London's historic Westminster Abbey, was made perhaps even more significant by one simple fact: unlike her groom, who was second in line for the British throne (after his father, Prince Charles), Kate was not herself royal. She was not even a member of England's **aristocracy**. It was the first time in more than 350 years that a direct heir to the throne had lawfully married a **commoner**.

Even so, Kate looked perfectly at ease. No doubt this was due in part to the years of preparation she had endured for this new role, having spent some eight years as William's girlfriend. It was also due to her natural grace, charm, and sense of style. It was never more evident than on her wedding day that, although Kate might be a commoner, she was far from common.

A Future Queen Is Born

Perhaps Kate's first and middle names—the queenly "Catherine" and "Elizabeth"—should have given some indication of her future role in British society. However, at her birth—on January 9, 1982 in Reading, England—no one could have imagined that Catherine Elizabeth Middleton would someday become royalty.

Clearly, Kate's middle-class parents would have had no inkling of their daughter's glittering future. Until her marriage on June 21, 1980, Kate's mother, Carole Elizabeth Middleton (née Goldsmith), worked as a flight attendant for British Airways. Carole, born in 1955 to builder Ronald Goldsmith and his wife Dorothy, was raised in a **council house** in Southall, a working-class suburb west of London. There, she attended the local **state school**. While on the job, Carole met Kate's father, Michael Francis Middleton, who worked as a steward and later as a flight dispatcher for British Airways. Michael, who was born in Leeds in 1949 to pilot Peter Middleton and his wife Valerie, was educated at Clifton College, a preparatory school in Bristol.

Like her parents, Kate's earlier ancestors—who ranged from solicitors and manufacturers in Leeds, to working-class laborers in London, to miners from Sunderland and County Durham, with a sprinkling of authors and actors in between—would have never dared dream that one of their own would ascend the social ladder as Kate would go on to do.

From Miners to Manufacturers

On her mother's side, several of Kate's forefathers were coal miners, performing difficult, dirty, dangerous, and sometimes even deadly work. While working in the "pit," as mines were called, miners might face fires, explosions, or rock slides. They might be run over by a coal-carrying tram, kicked to death by a horse, fall down a shaft, or drown.

Life for Kate's paternal ancestors was somewhat more comfortable. Kate's great-great-great-grandfather, William Middleton, worked as a solicitor in Leeds, as did her great-great grandfather, John, and great-grandfather, Noel. All three men earned a good living. Noel's fortunes were further improved by his marriage to Olive Lupton, who hailed from a wealthy Leeds family.

In short order, the Middleton family grew. On September 6, 1983, Kate's sister, Philippa "Pippa" Charlotte Middleton, arrived. Just nineteen months apart, Pippa and Kate would grow up to be great friends. On April 15, 1987, the family welcomed a baby boy, James. He would complete the Middleton family.

Kate's Early Years

Kate, who was called "Catherine" as a child, would go on to inhabit one of the world's most luxurious palaces, Kensington Palace. However, her first home was considerably more modest: a semi-detached Victorian in the village of Bradfield Southend, in Berkshire, which her parents had purchased in 1979 for $56,700 (£34,700).

Despite its proximity to Greater London, Berkshire is rural in nature, characterized by leafy lanes, picturesque villages, and scenic views of the River Thames. Berkshire is also known for its close royal ties: Windsor Castle, the oldest and largest occupied castle in the world and the official residence of Queen Elizabeth II, lies within its borders, as does Ascot, home of the famous Royal Ascot horse meet.

Schoolgirl Kate

In her early years, Kate attended St. Peter's Preschool with the other village children. In 1986, however, she commenced studies at St. Andrew's School, a preparatory institution in nearby Pangbourne. She would remain there until 1995. Pippa followed two years later. School

A young Kate Middleton at St. Andrew's School, in Pangbourne.

policy dictated that the girls wear a uniform consisting of a kilt, a white shirt, a green blazer, and a crested tie. Kate loved school so much, she told her mother she wanted to be a teacher when she grew up.

While at St. Andrew's School, Kate—who was above average in height—excelled at sports. In particular, she enjoyed swimming, hockey, tennis, **rounders** (a game that is played with a ball and a bat, similar to baseball), basketball, volleyball, badminton, and **netball** (similar to basketball). Most impressively, she set the school record in her age group in the high jump.

Kate also participated in public speaking competitions, debates, poetry recitals, and drama productions. In an interesting case of foreshadowing, Kate, at age ten starred as Eliza Doolittle in *My Fair Lady*. A musical based on the book *Pygmalion* by George Bernard Shaw, the story is about a Cockney girl who takes speech lessons so that she might pass as a well-born lady.

It was at St. Andrew's that Kate first laid eyes on her future husband, Prince William. Ten-year-old Kate was among several St. Andrew's students who sought to catch a glimpse of the nine-year-old prince—then a pupil at a nearby boarding school—who took part in a hockey match at St. Andrew's.

The Family Business

Soon after the birth of her son James, Carole Middleton had an idea. Raising three young children, she quickly found the work involved in planning parties for her children—and in assembling the gift bags that were distributed to partygoers as favors—to be taxing. Guessing that other moms were fed up with this chore, it occurred to Carole that she might be able to supplement the family's income, then limited to Michael's British Airways salary, by selling these gift bags to other moms. To that end, Carole launched Party Pieces.

Initially, Party Pieces was a mail-order operation run from the family's home. Carole gave out catalogs, often featuring photos of her children alongside her product line, to other moms in the village. In time, as the popularity of the Internet increased, Carole created a website for the company. She also expanded her offerings to include party supplies and decorations.

Party Pieces was, in a word, a goldmine. By 1995, the business had become so successful that Michael quit his job at British Airways to join the company, which relocated to a larger space to accommodate more stock and employees.

Moving to Bucklebury

As Party Pieces grew, so, too, did the wealth of the Middleton family. In time, they traded their family home in Bradfield Southend for a five-bedroom residence, called "Oak Acre," in the nearby village of Bucklebury. Set on one and a half acres of land and shielded by oak trees and mixed woodlands, the redbrick house, covered in vines

An Ancient Village: The History of Bucklebury

Situated on the banks of the River Pang, the village of Bucklebury dates back nearly a thousand years. The village is mentioned in the **Domesday Book**, written in 1086. (Commissioned by William the Conqueror, who led the **Norman Conquest** of Britain in 1066, the Domesday Book contains the results of a great land survey, listing the land and resources owned in England—some 13,418 places in all—for the purposes of taxation. In the Domesday Book, "Bucklebury" is referred to as Borgeldeberie.) The land on which the village is situated originally encircled a royal manor owned by Edward the Confessor, whose reign spanned from 1042 until the Norman Conquest. During the reign of King Henry I, Bucklebury—whose parish church is thought to have been built in the second half of the eleventh century (with numerous additions and modifications thereafter)—was granted to the Reading Abbey, which housed monks of the Cluniac order. The Reading Abbey retained the land until the **Dissolution of the Monasteries** in 1540, when the order was forced to surrender it to King Henry VIII.

and wisteria, was accessible only by a private lane. The family would live at Oak Acre for many years to come.

Kate quickly adapted to life in her new village, just a few miles from her first home in Bradfield Southend.

On weekends, village residents frequently spotted Kate and her siblings taking long walks, soaking in the historic village and countryside.

Boarding School Bound

With the move to Bucklebury came other changes, most notably, Kate's transfer to Downe House, a girl's boarding school in nearby Cold Ash. Kate—then thirteen years old—spent only two terms at the new school. Few know the exact reasons for her departure, but it is widely speculated that other students bullied her. Whatever the reason, Kate soon settled in at another boarding school, Marlborough College, an exclusive coeducational preparatory school in Wiltshire, some thirty miles (48 kilometers) from Bucklebury. Kate was homesick at first. Many of her classmates were the sons and daughters of British earls, dukes, and barons, so Kate may have felt out of place. However, she quickly adjusted to life at the **public school**.

Students at Marlborough College described Kate as "level-headed, popular, and talented." Her best friend and roommate, Jessica Hay, recalled,

"She didn't get involved in any drinking or smoking, but was very sporty instead and very family-oriented."

Kate's confidence likely grew when her sister, Pippa, joined her at the school.

While at Marlborough College, Kate studied Chemistry, Biology, and Art, ultimately passing her **A-levels** in each. She excelled in her studies to such a degree that she was made a **prefect**. Kate also played tennis, hockey, and netball, ran cross-country, and competed in the high jump. She even earned a **Duke of Edinburgh Gold Award** while at Marlborough College. Of course, she would have had no inkling the Duke of Edinburgh would later become her grandfather-in-law!

Becoming a Beauty

Because of Kate's active participation in various sports, she developed an athletic figure. Although she was thought to be "skinny" at one time, she blossomed during the summer of 1998, when she was sixteen years old. One student noted,

"Catherine came back after the long summer break... an absolute beauty."

As a blossoming young woman, she began taking more care with her appearance, a task that included applying makeup (albeit sparingly). Her style of dress was conservative—jeans and sweaters with discreet accessories.

Kate blossomed
during her years
at Marlborough
College.

Not surprisingly, Kate had many male admirers at Marlborough College. Even so, she was not yet terribly interested in boys. Although it's believed that she did have a boyfriend or two, these relationships were not serious. Friends described her as "quite old fashioned," noting

> *"She wanted to save herself for someone special."*

Kate's Gap Year Abroad

After completing her studies at Marlborough College in July of 2000, Kate embarked on a gap year. Many British teens take a gap year—that is, a break between secondary school (high school) and higher education (university). Her first stop: Florence, Italy, where she attended a twelve-week course at the British Institute on Italian art. Art was a particular passion of Kate's; she would go on to major in art history at university. Kate, by then eighteen years old, enjoyed exploring the town, photographing its many architectural and artistic wonders. Following her time in Italy, Kate flew to Patagonia, Chile, where she did volunteer work. (Coincidentally, Prince William would do the same.) She also crewed on a boat in the Solent, the strait separating the Isle of Wight from the mainland of England, and spent time abroad with her family.

At the conclusion of her gap year, Kate was no doubt ready for the next phase of her life: university. Given her success at Marlborough College, her options were many. In the end, she chose the University of St. Andrews in Scotland. Steeped in history, the picturesque St. Andrews would prove the right choice for Kate. Not only would she enjoy and excel at her studies, she would also meet her future husband, the future King of England.

CHAPTER TWO

Attending St. Andrews and Meeting Prince William

In September 2001, Kate embarked on the next phase of her life: studying art history at the University of St. Andrews. Founded in 1413, St. Andrews is the oldest university in Scotland and the third oldest in the English-speaking world. Since its founding, the university has played host to numerous great minds, including many scientists, philosophers, and writers.

Kate quickly settled into her small garret in St. Salvator's Hall—"Sally's" for short—one of the university's eleven residence halls. Not far from Sally's was the center of the town of St. Andrews. Composed of just three main streets, St. Andrews was teeming with eager undergrads. The students, Kate included, enjoyed exploring the town's fashionable cafes, quaint shops, and lively pubs. It was in this out-of-the-way corner of Scotland that Kate would meet her future husband, Prince William.

The Arrival of William Wales

While most first-year students arrived the same day as Kate, one student waited. That student was nineteen-year-old Prince William, who had enrolled at St. Andrews under the name William Wales. Wary of **paparazzi** and mindful of his role in life, William sought to avoid attention by eschewing Freshers' Week, an orientation period that often turned raucous. Even so, when William arrived at St. Andrews, more than 3,000 well-wishers—students and town residents alike—turned out to welcome him.

Prince William Arrives at St. Andrews

Traditionally, members of the royal family attend Oxford or Cambridge, but William was drawn to St. Andrews' four-year course in art history, considered among the best in the nation. He also relished the landscape. William's grandmother, Queen Elizabeth II, was delighted with William's choice. This was due in part to St. Andrews' proximity to Balmoral, a royal estate that she visited often, a mere two hours' drive away.

Like Kate, William was assigned to St. Salvator's Hall. William's room in Sally's, however, boasted a bombproof door and bulletproof windows. His quarters had also been fitted with a small bathroom with reinforced walls, which could be used as a shelter in case of emergency. In addition, William's protection officers were housed just down the corridor.

About Prince William

When Kate arrived at St. Andrews, she was likely already acquainted with a few of her fellow students, but was relatively unknown. This was not the case for William. All of Great Britain—in fact, the whole world—had watched the prince grow up. After all, he is the heir to the throne of England.

Prince William Arthur Philip Louis, nicknamed "Wombat" by his family, was born on June 21, 1982, to Prince Charles and his wife, Diana, Princess of Wales. William was an instant celebrity. Thousands of Britons gathered outside Buckingham Palace, as well as outside St. Mary's Hospital in London, where William was born, to await news of his arrival. The entire nation was obsessed with photos of Charles and Diana holding the newborn prince.

Two years later, on September 15, 1984, William's younger brother, Harry, was born. William and Harry—dubbed "the heir and the spare" by the press—would grow up to be the closest of friends.

Princess Diana was determined to give William and Harry as normal a life as possible. Rather than educating the boys at home, as was the tradition among royals, she sent both boys to a day school near Kensington Palace. She even made a point of taking them herself rather than delegating the task to a nanny. In 1987, at age five, William switched to the nearby Wetherby School. Three years later, at age eight, William was sent to boarding school at Ludgrove. Harry followed two years later.

Ludgrove offered William and Harry a respite from what had become a difficult home life. Their parents' marriage was quickly falling apart, and the London press saw fit to publish countless stories on the matter. Officials at Ludgrove took great care to shelter the boys from what had become an untenable situation, as did administrators at Eton College, where William transferred in 1995 at the age of thirteen. (Harry would join him there three years later.)

At Eton, William enjoyed studying English, history, and foreign languages. He received 'A' grades in each.

A Brief History of Eton College

Eton College—Eton for short—has a long and storied history. Founded by Henry VI in 1441, the school, located near Windsor Castle, is a haven for the sons of England's aristocracy. It boasts countless notable graduates, called "Old Etonians." These include nineteen British Prime Ministers, countless authors, several actors, and numerous scientists, economists, and politicians.

He also enjoyed participating in such sports as swimming, soccer, rugby, and his favorite, water polo. He was accepted into Pop, a prestigious school society, which gave him the authority to dole out punishment to fellow students who broke the rules. He rarely did so, however. One classmate recalled, "William was pretty cool, and he wouldn't hand out detentions and punishments even though he could." Eton's proximity to Windsor Castle offered Prince William one extra benefit: the ability to visit his grandmother, Queen Elizabeth II, for Sunday tea—an outing he enjoyed regularly.

Princess Diana's Tragic Death

During William's time at Eton, tragedy struck. On August 31, 1997, William's mother, Diana—by then divorced from Prince Charles and stripped of her royal title—was tragically killed in an automobile accident while being chased by paparazzi.

William and Harry were devastated. Both had adored their mother, dubbed by then-Prime Minister Tony Blair "the people's princess." Even so, William and Harry did their royal duty. They marched from Kensington Palace to Westminster Abbey behind the **cortège** transporting their mother's body, accompanied by their father, Prince Charles; their uncle (Diana's brother), Charles, Earl Spencer; and their grandfather (Charles's father), Prince Philip, also known as the Duke of Edinburgh.

A heartbroken William (second from left) and Harry (second from right) follow their mother's cortège from Kensington Palace to Westminster Abbey. Also pictured: Prince Philip; Charles, Earl Spencer; and Prince Charles.

Years later, William's brother Harry would speak of their mother's "unrivaled love of life, laughter, fun, and folly." He would go on to say that she was "our guardian, friend and protector. She never once allowed her unfaltering love for us to go unspoken or undemonstrated. She will always be remembered for her amazing public work. But behind the media glare, to us, just two loving children, she was quite simply the best mother in the world." Cheekily, he added, "We would say that, wouldn't we? But we miss her."

Settling In at St. Andrews

Four years after his mother's death, William arrived at St. Andrews. There, as everywhere, he simply wanted to be treated like everyone else. Thanks to an agreement struck by his father with the press, who promised to leave William be in exchange for the occasional official interview, William was able to move freely about St. Andrews. It didn't hurt that university officials also required each student to sign a confidentiality agreement upon enrolling, promising not to speak to reporters about the prince. For the first time in his young life, William could shop at the local grocery store and buy bonbons from a nearby candy shop.

Naturally, William encountered Kate Middleton during his early days at St. Andrews. After all, in addition to living in the same residence hall, both focused their studies on art history. Besides, Kate was hard to miss. At the close of Freshers' Week, she had been crowned prettiest girl at Sally's, and the boys on campus often referred to her as "Beautiful Kate." Unlike many of the girls at school who worked aggressively to catch the prince's eye, Kate was shy and quiet—something William appreciated. After their engagement, Kate recalled their first meeting:

"I actually think I went bright red when I met [him] and sort of scuttled off, feeling very shy."

In time, Kate's shyness eased. She soon began eating breakfast with the prince after her morning run. Sparks did not immediately fly between the pair, however. Kate had begun dating Rupert Finch, a charismatic law student. William also seemed to be clinging to the memory of a young woman named Arabella Musgrave, whom he had dated the summer before.

It wasn't just Arabella who William missed; he pined for all his friends back home. This partially explains why, when William went home for Christmas, he announced that he did not wish to return to St. Andrews. In addition to missing his friends, William also found that he was not interested in his coursework. Moreover, he deemed the workload too challenging. He also complained that St. Andrews was too far away.

Charles listened patiently to William's complaints, but suggested William give it another term. The Queen and Prince Philip concurred. "He needs to buckle down and not wimp out," Prince Philip remarked. One more voice chimed in: that of Kate Middleton. Kate and William had become close friends during their first term at St. Andrews. In the end, William relented—though he changed his major to geography— and both he and Kate returned to school on January 9, Kate's 20th birthday.

Friendship Blooms into Love

> *"When I first met Kate, I knew there was something very special about her."*

William was smitten with Kate at first glance. "We ended up being friends for a while and that was a good foundation."

Many believe that for William, friendship shifted into something more on March 27, 2002. On that day, Kate participated in a student-run charity fashion show. Wearing a sheer dress over a bandeau top and bikini bottom, Kate, who was normally quite demure in her dress, strode down the catwalk. William—who had paid $325 (£200) for a front-row seat, was gobsmacked.

Later that evening, at a party, William and Kate clinked glasses to toast Kate's success. William then leaned in for a kiss. Stunned, Kate, who was still in a relationship with Rupert Finch and considered William no more than a friend, pulled away.

During their second year at St. Andrews, Kate and William, still close friends, shared a **flat** in the center of town with two other friends, Fergus Boyd and Olivia Bleasdale. Each paid $165 (£100) a week in rent and shared in cooking and cleaning tasks. William was relegated to trash duty, and Kate regularly made supper

Kate Middleton struts the catwalk at a charity fashion show.

for the group. Naturally, security measures were taken. Like William's dorm room, the flat was fitted with bulletproof windows and a bombproof front door. A state-of-the-art security system was also installed.

Eventually, Kate broke things off with Rupert. She and William became a couple, and over time their love grew. Kate found that she had much in common with the young prince. Both loved the outdoors, and enjoyed drama and sports. They often played tennis together, and on many occasions Kate joined William for a vigorous early-morning swim. Perhaps most importantly, she was not overly dazzled by William's royal pedigree. When one friend commented on her luck in landing William, Kate quickly retorted,

"He's lucky to be going out with me!"

While their romance was considered an open secret among their group at St. Andrews, William and Kate sought to keep it under the radar for those outside their circle. That meant engaging in elaborate cover-ups and using decoys. They never left the house at the same time, and they took care to arrive separately at parties. They also agreed never to hold hands in public.

They remained secretive about their relationship partly because of William's contempt for the **Fourth Estate**, or the press, due in no small part to the role it had played in his parents' divorce and his mother's tragic death. Moreover, William sought to protect Kate from the harsh glare of public life.

Their cloak of privacy would remain intact until 2004 when *The Sun*, a London tabloid, published photos of Kate and William on vacation at a ski resort in Switzerland. Those photos brought to an end all speculation about the nature of William and Kate's relationship.

When photos of Kate and William on a ski holiday in 2004 leaked, speculation that the two were in a relationship was confirmed.

Graduation... and a New Beginning

On June 23, 2005, just two days after William's twenty-third birthday, William and Kate graduated from St. Andrews. William earned a degree in geography, while Kate's was in art history. The ceremony was well attended and included such luminaries as Queen Elizabeth II, Prince Philip, Prince Charles, and his new wife, Camilla. Armed with her diploma and looking stunning in a simple black skirt and white blouse, Kate looked forward to her future—with the future King of England.

A stunning Kate Middleton graduates from St. Andrews University.

CHAPTER THREE

Adjusting to Life in the Public Eye

At St. Andrews, Kate and William lived in a protective bubble. In London, where Kate moved after graduation, that bubble burst. Navigating her new life—one in which she was besieged by paparazzi as her beloved William pursued a career in the military—was a challenge. Nevertheless, it was a challenge that Kate would meet head on.

Finding Work

Like most university graduates, Kate was keen to begin a career, but she also had her relationship with William to consider. She needed a job that allowed her some privacy, as well as the flexibility to visit William—who had entered the military—on a regular basis.

Her first attempt at a career was to start a children's clothing business, but she soon decided the idea was unsound. As her next career move, Kate accepted a job as an accessories buyer for a chain of clothing stores called Jigsaw.

Kate loved the job. And the company's owner, Belle Robinson, had only good words to say about her famous employee. "I was so impressed by her," she commented. At work, Kate never acted like she was better than the others. Robinson recalled,

"She sat in the kitchen at lunchtime and chatted with everyone, from the van drivers to the accounts girls."

Unfortunately, constant harassment by the paparazzi and William's military obligations made a nine-to-five existence nearly impossible. Kate resigned from Jigsaw in 2007 and began working for her parents' company, Party Pieces. Kate, a keen photographer, designed the company's catalogues and marketing materials. She even took a course in graphic design to boost her creative skills.

Some people criticized Kate, saying she lacked drive and was merely a "princess-in-waiting." However, as one Middleton friend remarked, "She's been offered every job under the sun. Russian oligarchs, fashion designers— everyone wants her. But if she goes out and works, she'll be accused of abusing her connections—or of being used." The friend concluded, "What can she do? She's in a very difficult position."

Becoming a Style Icon

Due in part to the unceasing attention from the press, Kate had become a style icon. She was cited multiple times in *Vanity Fair* magazine's International Best-Dressed List and received similar honors from the *Daily Telegraph*, *Tatler*, and *People* magazine.

What is Kate's style? In a word: classic. Trendy clothes are not for Kate. She sticks to elegant, simple designs, favoring tailored blazers and boots. Over the years, her look has become more sophisticated. At St. Andrews, Kate was frequently seen in such wardrobe staples as boot-cut jeans, cashmere sweaters, and UGG boots. Since then, she has developed a sleeker style.

Kate makes a special effort to wear clothing by British designers in an attempt to call attention to their wares. Kate's **patronage** has helped a number of UK designers attract an international audience, thereby boosting their bottom line—something they call "the Kate effect."

Supporting William's Career Aspirations

Kate had more than her own career aspirations to think about. She had William's to consider as well. William, like his brother Harry, had chosen a career in the military. This was to prepare him to be king, as he would be required to lead the nation's armed forces. In 2005, William passed the Army's Regular Commission Board selection process. He was duly accepted into a forty-eight-week officer training program at the Royal Military Academy, Sandhurst, commencing in January of 2006.

At Sandhurst, Officer Cadet Wales, as William was known, enjoyed no special privileges despite his status as second in line for the throne. Major-General Andrew Ritchie noted, "I can assure you that he will be treated the same as every other cadet." By way of explanation, the Major-General noted that cadets "need to know what it is like to be tired and hungry, to lead their soldiers in demanding situations around the world."

During his first five weeks at Sandhurst, William was not permitted contact with family or friends—including Kate. He endured grueling days, rising at dawn and working late into the night. Once this basic training phase was over, however, William was permitted brief furloughs during the weekends. He and Kate regularly met at Prince Charles's estate, Highgrove, or at the Middletons' home in Bucklebury.

It was with great celebration that William graduated from Sandhurst in December of 2006. Kate and her parents were invited to witness the ceremony. It was only the second time that Kate would be in the official presence of William's grandmother, Queen Elizabeth

II. (The first was at her and William's graduation from St. Andrews.) Naturally, Kate sought to make a good impression. Her attire—a scarlet overcoat, complemented by black leather gloves and a black hat to protect her from the cold—certainly did so! Seated comfortably among the Prince's family, including the Queen, Prince Philip, Prince Charles, and Camilla, the Duchess of Cornwall, Kate stood out.

After Sandhurst, William would receive yet more military training. First, he spent five months training in Dorset. Then he joined the Household Cavalry regiment in Windsor. That included a four-month stint with the Royal Air Force (RAF) followed by a two-month stint with the Royal Navy. After that, William embarked on an eighteen-month training course with the Royal Air Force's Search and Rescue Force (SARF).

Kate, flanked by her parents, Michael and Carole Middleton, attends the Sovereign's Parade at the Royal Military Academy, Sanchurst, in 2006.

Prince William stifles a smile as his grandmother, Queen Elizabeth II, inspects the troops at Sandhurst.

He was shaping up to be a fine soldier—or, as Prince Charles affectionately called him, "combat wombat." On April 11, 2008, William "received his wings," qualifying as an RAF pilot. While Harry would see combat in Afghanistan, William—now called Flying Officer Wales—would be deemed too valuable to put in harm's way. This bothered him greatly—particularly when his squadron was sent to Afghanistan for a six-month deployment. Nonetheless, William found a way to serve his country with valor. In September of 2010, the prince was assigned to work as a search-and-rescue helicopter pilot in Anglesey, Wales.

For Kate, William's military service meant that he was away more often than not. Perhaps royal biographer Andrew Morton put it best when he wrote, "As she waited for her prince to come home, Kate realized that she had signed up for a life of long goodbyes, endless texting, and haphazard phone calls." Morton continued,

> *"All she could do, as a military wife in waiting, was adopt the wartime slogan 'Keep calm and carry on.'"*

Dealing with Paparazzi

Even in William's absence, Kate found herself hounded by paparazzi. These photographers knew they could command a pretty penny for any photographs of Kate, as sales skyrocketed anytime a newspaper or magazine published photos of the princess-in-waiting. For many —William included—the constant presence of the paparazzi brought painful reminders of Princess Diana, who had faced constant assaults by photographers. It was while fleeing from the press that the beautiful princess had been tragically killed.

Incredibly, Kate rarely seemed rattled by the cameras that had followed her day and night since her arrival in London. "She always smiles and never says a word," observed former royal press secretary Dickie Arbiter. That changed in the days leading up to Kate's twenty-fifth birthday. A rumor that Prince William planned to propose on her birthday—though completely unfounded—had begun to swirl. As a result, even more photographers than usual had set up camp outside Kate's Chelsea flat. By the morning of her birthday, on January 9, 2007, hundreds of photographers had mobbed her doorstop, all hoping for a pre-engagement photo. Due at work, Kate emerged from her flat and made for her car, whereupon she was swarmed by the press. As noted by journalist Vicky Ward, "It was the first and only time in her relationship with Prince William that the young woman seemed almost to lose her temper. Her usual smile was replaced by tightly closed lips, and her bluish-hazel eyes were stormy."

Bumps in the Road

In addition to being constantly harassed by paparazzi, Kate was subject to countless humiliations in the press. Kate and her sister, Pippa, by then a student at the prestigious Edinburgh University, were dubbed the "Wisteria Sisters"—meaning, according to *Tatler* magazine, they were "highly decorative, terribly fragrant and [had] a ferocious ability to climb." Worse, due to the prince's alleged refusal to propose marriage, the press had taken to referring to Kate as "Waity Katy," a degrading epithet.

It didn't help that many royal hangers-on sniggered about Kate's upbringing. Many of William's supposed friends amused themselves by shouting "doors to manual!" whenever the subject of Kate's mother, who had once been a British Airways flight attendant, arose. One member of William's aristocratic set criticized the Middletons for something as trivial as having a **tarmac** driveway. (In England, a tarmac driveway is seen as a sign of **new money**; in contrast, those with **old money** generally have gravel driveways.)

Many believed that Kate simply lacked the necessary "breeding" to become queen, deeming the Middletons "too middling" for the royal set. As one Scottish nobleman observed,

> "It was felt that she wasn't from the right stock... William was expected to find a suitable bride among the aristocracy or European royalty. One of his own kind. Kate was treated abominably behind her back by some who should have shown better manners."

Kate, besieged by the press on her twenty-fifth birthday.

Not surprisingly, all these pressures soon threatened to crush Kate and William's relationship. Increasing the strain was the fact that Kate clearly wanted William to commit to marriage, while William was less certain about the couple's future. This combination of woes led William to end their relationship in April of 2007, after nearly five years of courtship.

Kate was devastated. Kate's friend Emma Sayle recalled, "William was the love of her life." Sayle went on: "But she said the relationship was hard because they were constantly in the public eye." Clearly, Kate was not ready to give up on her prince. As noted by royal biographer Katie Nicholl, "[Kate] knew that by giving [William] time and space she could probably get him back, and she did so by being very clever, stepping out at his favorite clubs, looking glamorous and fabulous." She went on to say: "Her message to William was clear: 'Look what you're missing!'"

Reunited

To put it bluntly: message received. William quickly regretted his decision to split with Kate. Although their romance had sometimes been turbulent, Kate had always proved to be reliable and true. But it took some convincing before Kate agreed to see him again.

By late May, the couple were again an item, albeit in secret. They desperately needed time to themselves, away from the glare of the public eye. It was not until

Kate attended the Concert for Diana, which William and Harry had organized, but sat two rows behind her prince.

July 1, 2007, that the two were spotted in public, in the royal box during a concert that William and his brother Harry had organized to honor their late mother. Kate and William's status remained ambiguous, however, as Kate, smartly dressed in a white trench coat, wisely sat with her brother James two rows behind William.

Two months later, Kate and William flew to the Seychelles, a chain of islands in the Indian Ocean. During that trip, they discussed their future. As a member of their inner circle explained, "They didn't agree to get married there and then; what they made was a pact... He promised her his commitment and said he would not let her down, and she in turn agreed to wait for him."

Later, Kate would view their brief breakup as valuable. As Kate said,

> *"I think at the time I wasn't very happy about it, but actually it made me a stronger person. You find out things about yourself that maybe you hadn't realized."*

For his part, William chalked the experience up to a foolish, youthful mistake. "We were both very young," he explained. "We were both finding ourselves and being different characters. It was very much trying to find our own way and we were growing up so it was just a bit of space and it worked out for the better."

CHAPTER FOUR

A Royal Wedding

Kate and William had long endured speculation about when they would wed. In October of 2010, William finally popped the question, sparking a frenzy of interest and anticipation. How had William proposed? What did the ring look like? Where would the couple hold the service? When would it take place? And, perhaps most importantly, what would Kate wear?

The Proposal

Kate and William had discussed marriage for some time before William finally asked for her hand. The couple had made a pact to marry some years earlier. "Both of us have come to the decision pretty much together. I just chose when to do it and how to do it,"

William explained. He went on, tongue firmly in cheek: "Obviously being a real romantic I did it extremely well."

Indeed he did. William proposed while on holiday with Kate in Kenya. After a fruitless afternoon of fishing, William produced a ring from his pack. It fit Kate's finger perfectly. He asked for her hand, and Kate jubilantly assented. It had been eight years since she had fallen for young William Wales. At last, they were to be married.

The Ring

When the first photos of the newly engaged couple were released, royal watchers everywhere immediately recognized the ring that graced Kate's left hand. It had belonged to William's mother—presented to her by William's father, Prince Charles, upon their engagement. The famous ring, which Diana wore until her death, featured a glittering eighteen-carat oval sapphire encircled by a series of smaller diamonds. It had cost $41,122 (£25,000)—$411,225 (£250,000) in today's money—and had been purchased by the Queen.

Planning the Wedding

The young couple set a date for their big day: Friday, April 29, 2011. England's prime minister, David Cameron, quickly confirmed that the date would be considered a national holiday, meaning that many Britons would have the day off.

Unlike William's parents, who were married at St. Paul's Cathedral—an event watched by some 750 million people worldwide—Kate and William chose Westminster Abbey as their venue. This was due, according to palace aides, to its "staggering beauty, its thousand years of royal history, and its relative intimacy

A Brief History of Westminster Abbey

Westminster Abbey has a rich history. In the middle of the tenth century, Benedictine monks worshipped at the site. During the eleventh century, King Edward built a large stone church on the site in honor of St. Peter the Apostle. This church became known as the "west minster" (in contrast to St. Paul's Cathedral, known as the "east minster")—hence its name, Westminster Abbey. Construction of the church that exists on the site today was begun in 1245 by King Henry III.

Considered an architectural masterpiece in the Gothic style, the Abbey is the final resting place of some 3,000 people—including seventeen kings and queens—as well as shrines and memorials to countless famous historical figures, including statesmen, scientists, warriors and writers.

Westminster Abbey—a veritable treasure trove of paintings, stained glass, textiles, and other artifacts— has been the setting of every **coronation** since 1066, when William the Conqueror was crowned King of England, and of sixteen royal weddings (including Kate and William's).

despite its size." It was in this church that William's grandparents Queen Elizabeth II and the Duke of Edinburgh had been married more than sixty years before. The church had also been the location of countless coronations—including Queen Elizabeth II's—and state funerals. It was at Westminster Abbey that the funeral for William's mother, Princess Diana, was held.

The Big Day Arrives

The day of Kate and William's wedding was quickly upon them. The whole world was breathless in anticipation. At the same time, royal watchers were also deeply nostalgic, remembering when the young Lady Diana Spencer had married her prince, William's father, nearly thirty years before.

William's parents, Diana and Charles, on their wedding day.

Unlike Diana, Kate broke from tradition, traveling to Westminster Abbey via limousine rather than an open carriage. En route, Kate, accompanied by her father, was met with cheers and shouts from more than a million spectators.

At precisely 11 a.m., Kate arrived at the Abbey and emerged from the vehicle. Her dress—the details of which had been a closely guarded secret—was then revealed to the more than two billion people watching worldwide. Designed by Sarah Burton of Alexander McQueen, a famous British fashion house, the ivory gown was stunning. The top featured sleeves and a V-neck of sheer lace over a form-fitting bodice. The skirt, made of silk satin gazar, was full with a long train. Royal biographer Andrew Morton described the gown as, "elegant, understated, beautifully balancing tradition with modernity, [and] quintessentially feminine."

Kate's makeup, which she had done herself, was subtle. Over her hair, which was styled in an elegant demi-chignon, Kate wore a lace-edged veil. It was held in place by a diamond Cartier tiara on loan from the Queen. (The Queen had offered Kate her choice of three tiaras from the royal collection; Kate, true to form, chose the simplest and most understated one.) Kate's earrings, a gift from her parents, were custom made to match the tiara. The dangling diamond baubles featured an acorn motif, reflecting the Middleton family's newly minted **coat of arms**. As for Kate's bouquet, it was surprisingly humble, composed of ivy, hyacinth, myrtle, and, fittingly, sweet William.

Kate, resplendent in her Alexander McQueen gown, prepares to enter Westminster Abbey. She is aided by her sister, Pippa.

The services of Kate's maid of honor, her sister, Pippa, were immediately needed to wrangle the train. For her part, Pippa was suitably stunning. Like her sister's, Pippa's gown was designed by Sarah Burton of Alexander McQueen. It was considerably less dramatic, however.

The Ceremony

It was a long walk from the Abbey's Great West Door to William, who waited at the altar—four minutes to be exact. On her way to her groom, Kate passed by each of the 1,900 guests, including royals, diplomats, politicians, and celebrities. But it wasn't just luminaries in attendance. Also present were the butcher, postman, and others from Kate's village in Berkshire.

The Abbey itself was nearly as breathtaking as Kate. It had been filled with some 30,000 flowers. The church even featured a copse of maple trees, transforming it into a forest-like space. Orange-blossom candles scented the air.

Remarkably, Kate remained poised and composed—although her father appeared to falter while escorting his eldest daughter down the aisle. ("Please, Daddy, don't cry. It will set me off, too," Kate told him.) "You're so beautiful," William said when she finally arrived by his side. William—himself handsomely clad in his striking scarlet military uniform—was clearly bowled over by his bride.

With that, the ceremony got underway. Although Kate had received lessons in **elocution** in preparation for this moment, her voice trembled as she spoke her vows.

She promised to "love, comfort, honor, and keep" her husband, but notably omitted "obey." She also uttered William's Christian names, "William Arthur Philip Louis," correctly.

Soon enough, Kate and William, now wearing Welsh gold wedding bands on their fingers, were married. Kate had entered Westminster Abbey a commoner, but emerged from the church a noblewoman: Her Royal Highness The Duchess of Cambridge, Countess of Strathearn, and Lady Carrickfergus. The happy couple proceeded out of the Abbey to greet the waiting crowd outside.

Newly married, William and Kate proceed from Westminster Abbey. William's brother, Harry, and Kate's sister, Pippa, are visible behind them.

Greeting the Crowd

During their brief carriage ride from Westminster Abbey to the Queen's London home, Buckingham Palace, crowds of well-wishers cheered them on. "Are you happy?" Kate asked her husband. "Very," William replied, taking his wife's hand. He added, "This is mad. Gosh, the noise!"

When Kate and William arrived at the palace, it was time to greet the crowd in earnest. At 1:25 p.m., the couple, along with the rest of the royal family, the Middleton clan, and the wedding party, stepped onto the balcony at Buckingham Palace to deafening applause. "Oh, wow!" Kate exclaimed. Looking radiant, confident, and happy, she flashed a smile at her future subjects. "We want Kate! We want Kate!" they cheered in return. The spectators made a terrible racket—so much so that one young member of the bridal party, three-year-old Grace van Cutsem, grumpily covered her ears with her hands.

At his own wedding, Prince Charles had famously asked his mother "May I?" before kissing the ravishing Diana. This was not so for William, who eagerly kissed his bride. When the crowd demanded more—"Kiss! Kiss! Kiss!" they chanted—William turned to Kate and said, "Let's give them another one. I love you." Six minutes later—after a stunning fly-by of various World War II vintage aircraft and modern fighter jets—it was over. The Queen retreated indoors, and the rest of the group followed suit.

Kate and William greet well-wishers from the balcony at
Buckingham Palace.

The Celebration Continues...

Indoors, Kate and William enjoyed a champagne
reception prepared by a team of twenty-one chefs.
Hosted by the Queen, it was attended by some 650
guests. Everyone cheered when William introduced Kate
as "my wife, Mrs. Wales." He went on to describe her as a
"wonderful girl" and declared his love for her. Charles, too,
spoke well of Kate, noting that he was very lucky to now
have a daughter-in-law like her.

Next, the pair left for Clarence House, the London
residence of Prince Charles and the Duchess of
Cornwall, for some downtime. William drove his new

Vintage World War II aircraft perform a fly-by over Buckingham Palace as swarms of well-wishers congregate outside the palace gates.

bride in his father's vintage blue Aston Martin Volante, which had been decorated with a trail of balloons. The car's license plate read "JU5T WED" and featured an "L" mark, indicating the driver was merely a learner—most likely thanks to William's mischievous brother, Harry.

At six o'clock, it was time for Kate and William to prepare for the evening of dining and dancing at Buckingham Palace. William donned a tuxedo and Kate slipped into yet another Alexander McQueen gown—this one a strapless white dress with a diamanté waist—and an angora-wool bolero jacket. This gathering was yet more intimate than the last, with 300 of the couple's closest family and friends.

After dinner came more toasts. Harry went first, referring to William and Kate as "the Dude and the

Duchess." He described Kate as being "like a sister" to him, and remarked on how proud his mother would have been to see her eldest son so well settled. Kate's father, Michael, also spoke.

Just before midnight, Harry led the guests to the Throne Room, which had been transformed into a disco. Kate and William immediately took to the dance floor for a rendition of "Your Song," written by Sir Elton John and performed by Ellie Goulding. Soon, everyone joined them for a night of dancing and fun. Finally, at 2:30 a.m., everyone filed outside for a fireworks display. Kate and William then retired to Buckingham Palace's Belgian Suite, which is reserved for visiting royals.

The Honeymoon

Two weeks after their memorable wedding, Kate and William departed for their honeymoon. The couple had kept their plans secret in an attempt to outfox the media. Eventually, however, it was revealed that they had chosen a destination they'd visited before: the Seychelles. Situated in the Indian Ocean between the Equator and the Tropic of Capricorn, the **archipelago** of 115 islands, known for their lovely weather, white-sand beaches, and coconut groves, was the ideal getaway for the newlyweds, offering complete privacy. For William and Kate, it was the culmination of a perfect wedding—and the start of their new life as husband and wife.

CHAPTER FIVE

Becoming a Royal

In one fell swoop, Kate Middleton was transformed from a commoner to Her Royal Highness The Duchess of Cambridge, Countess of Strathearn, and Lady Carrickfergus. But it wasn't just her name that changed. With her marriage to Prince William, Kate was now a *bona fide* member of the royal family— "The Firm," as it is sometimes called—with all the rights and responsibilities that it entailed.

William realized that Kate might need help coping with the transition from commoner to royal. To that end, William enlisted **courtiers** to counsel her. One such advisor was Sir David Manning, who had once served as Great Britain's ambassador to the United States. Sir Manning instructed Kate in such matters as protocol and the ins and outs of royal life. William's stepmother Camilla, as well as his aunt, Sophie, Countess of Wessex—who had herself been born a commoner—also helped Kate navigate these new waters. For her part, Kate was naturally nervous about assuming her new royal identity.

"It's quite a daunting prospect, but hopefully I'll take it in my stride."

She added, "And William's a great teacher, so hopefully he will be able to help me."

Kate's Future Titles

When William's father, Prince Charles, ascends to the throne—which will likely occur upon the death of his mother, Queen Elizabeth II—William will become the Prince of Wales. In turn, Kate will become the Princess of Wales. That title belonged to William's mother, Diana, and is now held by Prince Charles' wife, Camilla (although she does not use it out of respect for Diana). Camilla's other title, Duchess of Cornwall, will also pass to Kate upon Charles's ascension. When Prince William becomes king—which will occur upon the death of his father—Kate will become the Queen Consort. As such, she will be known as Queen Catherine. Although she will be queen in name, she will never rule England. That right will be passed down to her oldest child.

Settling Into Married Life

In addition to adapting to her new identity as a royal, Kate also faced a task familiar to any new wife: getting used to married life. For Kate, that involved officially moving in with William in Anglesey, an island off the northwest coast of Wales, where William was stationed as a search-and-rescue helicopter pilot with the Royal Air Force (RAF).

Life in Anglesey was idyllic. Kate and William lived in a rustic, secluded four-bedroom farmhouse on the grounds of a country estate, well hidden from paparazzi. Villagers gave Kate and William a wide berth, allowing them to go about their days in peace. Kate was frequently spotted at the local supermarket or riding on the back of William's Ducati motorcycle. The couple frequently enjoyed taking in movies at the village cinema and dining at local pubs. As noted by one royal aide, Kate and William "absolutely loved their time in Anglesey and the company of the locals. They've been left alone and they have had an amazing time in Wales. The seclusion and the locals have made it very special."

While no one would have batted an eye if Kate and William had surrounded themselves with a large domestic staff—people to cook, clean, and otherwise tend to them—they opted against doing so. (That being said, they did finally hire a housekeeper to attend to certain household duties. And, of course, the couple is guarded by protection officers.) Kate also decided to eschew the tradition of appointing **ladies-in-waiting**—at least for the time being. To keep her company while William was at work, the couple adopted a black cocker spaniel puppy, which they named Lupo.

Picking Up the Royal Mantle

Although Kate and William loved their life in Anglesey, it would not be their permanent home. Their presence on the island was thanks to Queen Elizabeth II, who had agreed to give the couple a two-year grace period before entering royal life. This was to enable William to serve as a search-and-rescue pilot and to allow Kate a chance to adapt to life in "The Firm." At the conclusion of that period, both Kate and William would be expected to shift their focus to performing their royal duties on a full-time basis.

Chief among these duties is making public appearances in and around Great Britain and other countries in the **British Commonwealth**. Now called the Commonwealth of Nations, the British Commonwealth consists of fifty-three member states, most of which were at one time territories under the former British Empire. Member states include Canada, Australia, New Zealand, Barbados, Jamaica, and India. For example, royals often attend openings of hospitals and schools and lend a hand in times of crisis. Members of the royal family also often participate in military ceremonies and civic celebrations.

Kate and William's Coat of Arms

The Middleton's coat of arms (left), and Kate's impaled coat of arms (right), which blends her family's crest with William's.

Prior to Kate's marriage to William, the Middleton family was granted its own coat of arms. Sometimes called a family crest, a coat of arms is an emblem that represents a family. Upon her marriage to William, Kate was granted an **impaled coat of arms** for her own use. It blends into a single shield the Middleton family coat of arms with William's, which was given to him by his grandmother for his eighteenth birthday. In 2013, Kate and William were also granted a **conjugal coat of arms**, which represents both Kate and William. It features William's coat of arms alongside that of the Middleton clan rather than blended into a single shield. At the top is a crown, symbolizing that William is the heir apparent to the throne.

And of course, members of the monarchy participate in a great number of charitable activities.

In the course of their duties, royals often meet other world luminaries. During a tour of North America in 2011, Kate met many Hollywood celebrities, including Jennifer Lopez and Nicole Kidman. Kate also met the first lady of the United States, Michelle Obama, that same year.

Finding Purpose Through Charity

Members of the royal family have long lent their support to charities through formal patronages. Between them, members of the royal family currently support some 3,000 charities on a formal basis. Patronage by a member of the monarchy can help promote good causes.

Most patronages reflect the interest of their patron. For example, William's father, Prince Charles, is very interested in the environment, as well as in farming, gardening, and food. As such, he supports many charities that relate to these issues. The late Diana, Princess of Wales, was passionate about children, and was known for her extensive charity work on their behalf. Diana also worked tirelessly for charities focused on eradicating AIDS. For his part, William has partnered with his brother, Harry, to create a foundation that supports their favorite charities. These tend to focus on one of three areas: the armed forces, youth, and conservation. William also serves as patron for several charities that aid the homeless.

When Kate married William, she, too, became involved in his foundation. She also elected to become the royal patron of several additional charities—currently seven. She chose organizations that reflect her love of the arts and of sports, and her wish to work with children. Kate has said of her charity work:

> *"I really hope I can make a difference, even in the smallest way."*

One charity that was particularly close to Kate's heart was the Scout Association, which helps "young people in the UK enjoy new adventures, to experience the outdoors, interact with others, gain confidence, and have the opportunity to reach their full potential." As a patron of the Scout Association, Kate, who was a Brownie Scout

Kate volunteers on a Scout Association outing in the Lakes District.

in her youth, even volunteered at scouting functions in her area. As a result of her efforts, the Scout Association quickly saw a huge increase in adult volunteers, prompting a nod from Prince Charles: "I need hardly say that I am particularly delighted that my daughter-in-law has helped to swell the ranks of much-needed Scout volunteers."

Kate's interest in art was also reflected in her choices: The Art Room and, like Diana before her, the National

Kate and a budding artist at an Art Room facility.

Portrait Gallery. The Art Room, a small charity based in Oxford, uses art therapy to help troubled children ages five to sixteen raise their self-esteem, confidence, and independence. Since its inception in 2002, The Art Room has provided art therapy to more than 10,000 children and young people. The founder and director of the charity, Juli Beattie, noted of Kate's patronage: "The difference

[Kate] has made already is incalculable." For its part, the National Portrait Gallery boasts the most extensive collection of portraits on the planet. These include paintings, sculptures, photographs, and videos, with artists ranging from Holbein to Hockney and beyond. The gallery even includes a portrait of Kate herself!

In addition, Kate lent her support to East Anglia's Children's Hospices (EACH), which cares for children and young people with life-threatening conditions; Place2Be, which provides school-based mental health support for children; Action on Addiction, which disarms addiction through treatment, research, family support, education, and training; and the National History Museum, which seeks to inspire enjoyment in the natural world and responsibility for the future of our planet. SportsAid, which "helps the next generation of British sports stars by giving them financial support and recognition during the critical early years of their careers," has also received Kate's patronage.

Staying Close with the Middletons

Although royal life keeps Kate and William busy, they make time to visit with the Middletons as often as possible. Kate has always been particularly close with her mother, Carole. They enjoy visiting art galleries and shopping. The youthful Carole, often mistaken for Kate's sister, frequently advises Kate on the latest trends and styles. Yet, Kate finds that she is more like her father, Michael.

"She gets a lot of her characteristics from him," said one family friend. "Kate's feet are still on the ground, largely because of Michael. He doesn't get too swept up in the grandeur of her new life, and Kate loves him for that."

Of course, Kate looks forward to spending time with her siblings, Pippa and James, too. They are often invited on royal shooting weekends in Scotland. James, it is said, is a particularly good shot. Kate, William, Pippa, and James also enjoy playing tennis together.

Soon, there would be one more member of the Middleton clan: Kate and William were poised to welcome a royal baby into the family!

Kate's Portrait at the National Portrait Gallery

On display at London's National Portrait Gallery is a relatively new painting: one of Kate! The portrait, commissioned by the National Portrait Gallery, was painted by artist Paul Emsley.

At its unveiling in early 2013, the portrait met negative reviews. Said one critic: "He made her look older than she is and her eyes don't sparkle in the way that they do and there's something rather dour about the face." Another felt even more strongly: "Ghastly ... rotten ... an out and out disaster."

Not everyone agreed, however. Alistair Adams, president of the Royal Society of Portrait Painters, observed of the painting: "It's quite natural, it's open, it's straightforward and very pure. It's immediate and not overly sentimental." Perhaps most importantly, Kate and William loved the portrait. "I thought it was brilliant. It's just amazing," Kate told Emsley. Her husband concurred: "It's beautiful, it's absolutely beautiful."

This portrait of Kate hangs in the National Portrait Gallery.

CHAPTER SIX

The Birth of an Heir

In December of 2012, palace aides thrilled royal watchers everywhere by delivering an exciting piece of news: Kate and William were expecting their first child. This announcement caught the world somewhat by surprise. No one had detected even so much as a small bump on Kate's belly.

It was soon revealed that Kate was not yet through her first trimester. This was unusual, as many expectant mothers wait until they are farther along before sharing news of their condition. In Kate's case, her pregnancy was revealed because she had suffered hyperemesis gravidarum, or severe morning sickness. Her illness was so grave that she had been admitted to London's King Edward VII Hospital for treatment, where she remained for three days. Knowing this news might be leaked to the public, Kate and William decided to reveal it themselves.

Expectant Mum

In time, Kate's condition improved, and she was able to resume her royal duties. She was soon spotted wearing maternity clothes. Even while expecting, Kate—who affectionately referred to the bump on her belly as "our little grape"—remained stylish.

Even while pregnant, Kate remained stylish.

The fact that 2013 was one of England's hottest summers on record made life uncomfortable for Kate, especially as her due date—which she and William had kept private, but which the press suspected was sometime in mid-July—drew near. To escape their cottage in Anglesey, which had no air conditioning, Kate retreated to her parents' home in Bucklebury. The previous year, the Middletons had moved from Oak Acre to another home near the village. Called Bucklebury Manor, the seven-bedroom Georgian house featured a swimming pool, tennis court, and stunning gardens. To keep cool, Kate took frequent dips in the pool. She kept fit by practicing prenatal yoga and taking walks around the estate. On Saturday, July 20, Kate and William decamped to a cottage on the grounds of London's Kensington Palace in preparation for the birth, which was to take place in the city.

Labor Begins

On Monday, July 22, the "Great Kate Wait," as the press had dubbed her pregnancy, finally neared an end. Just before 6 a.m., Kate, in the early stages of labor, was admitted to the Lindo Wing at St. Mary's Hospital in west London—the very hospital in which Prince William had been born. To avoid the scrum of photographers and well-wishers camped outside the hospital in anticipation of their arrival, Kate and William accessed the hospital via a side entrance. A photographer, Mary Stanford, spotted them, but declined to photograph the moment. Stanford did describe it in words, however: "Kate was wearing a dark shawl and she had her hair down. She walked to the front door on her own, and that was it; she was in the hospital, the doors shut—it all happened in seconds. It was as if it had been rehearsed, it was so smoothly executed."

A short time later, the palace released a statement that Kate, with William at her bedside, was "in the early stages of labor." She was "doing well" and the birth was "progressing normally." As news of Kate's labor spread, delighted Brits mobbed the hospital and the gates of Buckingham Palace. Fans of the royal family and notable figures in Great Britain also took to social media to discuss the royal birth and send their greetings. The Archbishop of Canterbury tweeted, "My thoughts and prayers are with Kate on this enormously special day."

Naturally, the question on everyone's lips was, "Is it a boy or a girl?" Kate and William had chosen to keep the gender of their baby a surprise, even to themselves. Kate suspected she was carrying a son, while William was hoping for a daughter.

Welcoming the Future Monarch

At 4:24 p.m., after fourteen hours of labor, Kate and William welcomed their first child, a boy. He was a lovely baby, with a tuft of dark hair and, his proud father noted, "a good set of lungs." Kate described the birth, which had occurred naturally, as "perfect"—straight-forward, with no complications.

A Change in Succession Law

Since 1701, the crown of Great Britain had been passed to the eldest son of the current monarch upon his or her death or **abdication**, a practice called **male primogeniture**. If there was no son, the crown could pass to the eldest daughter. This was how William's grandmother, Elizabeth II, had inherited the throne. If the monarch had no children, the crown would pass to the monarch's oldest living brother. It was in this way that Elizabeth II's father, George VI, had become king; his elder brother, Edward VIII, had abdicated the throne in 1936 to marry American divorcée Wallis Simpson. If the monarch had no brothers, the crown passed to the oldest living sister.

In 2013, Great Britain changed the law of **succession**, adopting **absolute primogeniture**. Under the new law, Kate and William's first child would be eligible to ascend to the throne regardless of gender. This change was lauded by Prime Minister David Cameron, who noted, "The idea that a younger son should become monarch instead of an elder daughter simply because he's a man... this way of thinking is at odds with the modern countries that we've all become."

Weighing eight pounds and six ounces, the healthy baby boy—who was yet unnamed—was barely heavier than the crown that will one day grace his head. If, as expected, the baby's reign followed that of his grandfather, Prince Charles, and his father, Prince William, he would be the forty-third sovereign of England since William the Conqueror in 1066.

For just a few hours, Kate and William kept the news of their son's arrival quiet, sharing it only with family members. First was a call to William's grandmother, the Queen, on a specially encrypted phone. Then came calls to Kate's parents, sister, and brother, and to William's father, stepmother, and brother.

Finally, just before 8:30 p.m., Kate and William gave royal aides permission to release a statement announcing the birth. In a nod to modernity, the aides did so via e-mail and Twitter. The tweet read simply, "Her Royal Highness the Duchess of Cambridge was safely delivered of a son at 4:24 p.m." In keeping with tradition, however, an announcement of the prince's birth was also posted on an easel outside Buckingham Palace. The next morning, all the newspapers led with the birth of the infant prince. One publication, *The Sun*, even changed its masthead to read "The Son."

William gushed that he and Kate, both of whom remained in the hospital overnight with their infant son, "could not be happier." William, it was later revealed, had changed his son's first diaper. For his part, William's father, Charles, was "overjoyed at the arrival of my first grandchild."

Introducing George Alexander Louis, His Royal Highness Prince George of Cambridge

At 7 p.m. the next day, royal watchers caught their first glimpse of the young prince. Kate, looking remarkably fresh in a blue and white dress, and William brought their bundled baby outside. Kate, who had spent the day receiving visitors, including her parents, Prince Charles, and Camilla, Duchess of Cornwall, was nervous and feeling very emotional. Nevertheless, she appeared unflappable under the glare of the camera flashes. As noted by royal biographer Katie Nicholl, "With a winning smile and her wide, warm eyes, she absorbed the incredible spectacle before her." Nicholl noted that the baby

> *"As if on cue, stretched his tiny fingers in front of his crumpled face as though he were giving the world a wave."*

Later, William would say that he and Kate were "on such a high" during this display. They were in love with their new son. "We were happy to show him off to whoever wanted to see him."

Kate and William soon made public the name of their new baby. "The Duke and Duchess of Cambridge are delighted to announce that they have named their son George Alexander Louis," read a statement from Kensington Palace. "The baby will be known as His Royal Highness Prince George of Cambridge." Upon his ascension to the throne, he would become King George VII.

Adjusting to Motherhood

Following their stay in the hospital, Kate, William, and George stopped off for a night at Kensington Palace. There, George received a very important guest: his great grandmother, Queen Elizabeth II. "It was very typical of the Queen's thoughtfulness to go to them," observed one family member. William's brother Harry also had a chance to visit his new nephew. "When I saw him, he was crying his eyes out, like all babies do, I suppose." He added, teasingly, "I only hope my brother knows how expensive my babysitting charges are."

After Kensington Palace, the freshly minted family made for Bucklebury Manor. Kate longed to be home, in the bosom of her own family. Waiting for Kate, William, and George were Kate's parents, along with her sister, Pippa, and brother, James. The Middletons were, naturally, infatuated with the infant prince. Also on hand was Lupo, Kate and William's beloved dog.

At Bucklebury Manor, Kate enjoyed complete privacy. Visitors were kept to an absolute minimum, although Pippa and James dropped by frequently to see the new baby. Bucking royal protocol, Kate and William chose not to hire a nanny—at least not at first. "William said he didn't want a nanny or a nurse coming in and doing shifts," explained a friend. "They wanted to do the early days themselves." Kate and William did, however, accept help and guidance from Carole, who, in addition

Kate, George, William, and Lupo, along with the Middleton's beloved golden retriever, Tilly, at Bucklebury Manor. This official royal photograph, released by palace aides, was taken not by a famous photographer, but by Kate's father, Michael Middleton.

to helping to care for the baby, devoted much of her time to cooking healthy meals for Kate.

Soon, it was time for Kate and William to return to Anglesey. William had a few weeks left of his tour as a helicopter pilot remaining, after which he and Kate would move to London and resume their royal duties. Kate and William enjoyed this calm before the incoming storm, with William going to work each day while Kate stayed home to look after the baby. "I know both of us will miss it terribly when my search-and-rescue tour of duty comes to an end next month and we have to move elsewhere," William said.

Christening Prince George

On October 23, 2013, Prince George made his first public appearance: his christening at St. James's Palace. George, who was christened by the Archbishop of Canterbury, did not disappoint. Clad in a replica of the 172-year-old christening robe used by royal babies since the Victorian era, the future king smiled at family members, including his great grandparents, Queen Elizabeth II and Prince Philip.

William, George, and Kate on the day of George's christening.

The intimate ceremony was short but significant. Two hymns were sung, two lessons read, and two anthems were played. The archbishop made the sign of the cross on George's forehead and splashed water from the River Jordan on his head. The archbishop later said,

"As a nation we are celebrating the birth of someone who in due course will be the head of state. That's extraordinary. It gives you this sense of forward looking, of the forwardness of history as well as the backwardness of history, and what a gift to have this new life and to look forward."

Looking Forward

Looking forward is something that Kate and William will continue to do. It falls to them to bring modernity to the monarchy. "If [Kate and William] strike a balance between informality and royal tradition as they have thus far," noted royal biographer Katie Nicholl, "Prince George will have the very best of both worlds—a life of royal privilege, coupled with the same loving and comparatively ordinary family upbringing that Kate enjoyed and William always wanted."

For her part, Kate continues to adapt to royal life and motherhood. She has resumed her royal duties, making appearances for various charities and attending other events as a representative of the monarchy. She, William, and George have settled into their permanent family home, apartment 1A at Kensington Palace in London. The twenty-room spread—a few doors down from the apartment Princess Diana called home—has been refurbished specifically for them.

No doubt, Kate will continue to impress. Many liken her to the late Queen Mother, mother of Queen Elizabeth II. Like Kate, the Queen Mother was not born

The royal family and the Middleton clan on the day of George's christening. Front row, left to right: Queen Elizabeth II; Catherine, Duchess of Cambridge, with Prince George on her lap; Prince William. Back row, left to right: Prince Philip; Prince Charles; Camilla, Duchess of Cornwall; Prince Harry; Pippa Middleton; James Middleton; Carole Middleton; and Michael Middleton.

a royal, but she gained the love of the British people by always putting her royal duty above all else. As the older royals, such as Queen Elizabeth II and Prince Philip, scale back, it will fall to younger royals, such as Kate and William, to step up. There is little doubt that Catherine, Duchess of Cambridge, will heed that call.

Timeline

August 31, 1997

Princess Diana is tragically killed in an automobile accident in Paris

Fall, 2002

Kate and William begin dating, albeit secretly

December 2006

Kate and her parents attend William's graduation from Royal Military Academy Sandhurst

January 9, 1982

Catherine "Kate" Elizabeth Middleton is born to Carole and Michael Middleton

September 2001

Kate and William begin their studies at St. Andrews University

Summer, 2004

Kate and William split, but reconcile by the end of the year

Prince William is born to Prince Charles and Princess Diana

June 21, 1982

Kate participates in a student-run fashion show, where she catches William's eye

March 27, 2002

Kate and William graduate from St. Andrews

June 23, 2005

Kate completes her studies at Marlborough College

July 2000

A London tabloid, *The Sun*, publishes photographs of William and Kate on a ski vacation, making their romance known to the world

Spring, 2004

September 2007

Kate and William make a "marriage pact" while on vacation in the Seychelles

April 29, 2011

Kate and William are married in Westminster Abbey before a global audience of two billion people

October 23, 2013

Prince George s christened

May 2007

Kate and William reconcile, but keep their reconciliation a secret

October 2010

William proposes to Kate

December 2012

Royal aides announce that Kate and William are expecting their first baby, who will be heir to the throne

Kate and William are spotted in public at the Concert for Diana, organized by William and Harry to honor their mother, the late Princess Diana

July 1, 2007

Kate and William's engagement is announced to the public

November 2010

His Royal Highness Prince George Alexander Louis of Cambridge is born

July 22, 2013

William breaks up with Kate

April 2007

William is assigned to work as a search-and-rescue pilot in Anglesey, Wales. He and Kate will enjoy three years there, living in relative solitude

September 2010

Kate, William, and the rest of the royal family partake in celebrations for Queen Elizabeth II's Diamond Jubilee, marking her sixtieth year on the throne

June 2012

SOURCE NOTES

Chapter 1

P. 13, Witchell, Nicholas, "Royal Wedding: The Kate Middleton Story," www.bbc.co.uk/news/uk-11767308.

P. 13, Nicholl, Katie. *William and Harry: Behind the Palace Walls* (New York, NY: Weinstein, 2010), p. 157.

P. 14, Joseph, Claudia. *Kate: Kate Middleton: Princess in Waiting* (New York, NY: Avon, 2009), p. 135.

P. 16, Claudia, *Kate: Kate Middleton: Princess in Waiting*, p. 137.

Chapter 2

P. 23, Nicholl, *William and Harry: Behind the Palace Walls*, p. 92.

P. 24, Nicholl, *William and Harry: Behind the Palace Walls*, p. 223.

P. 25, "Prince William and Kate Middleton Talk About the Moment, the Ring, Children," http://abcnews.go.com/Entertainment/prince-william-kate-middleton-interview-transcript/story?id=12163826.

P. 26, Nicholl, *William and Harry: Behind the Palace Walls*, p. 140.

P. 27, "Prince William and Kate Middleton Talk About the Moment, the Ring, Children."

P. 29, Nicholl, *William and Harry: Behind the Palace Walls*, p. 147.

Chapter 3

P. 34, Ward, Vicky. "Will's Cup of Tea," www.vanityfair.com/style/features/2008/11/middleton200811.

P. 35, Ward, "Will's Cup of Tea."

P. 36, Morton, Andrew. *William & Catherine: A Royal Wedding* (New York, NY: St. Martin's, 2011), p. 125.

P. 39, Morton, *William & Catherine: A Royal Wedding*, p. 125.

P. 40, "Palace Advised Kate Middleton to Watch Footage of Diana for Tips on Dealing with Paparazzi," www.vanityfair.com/online/daily/2011/03/palace-advised-kate-middleton-to-watch-footage-of-diana-for-tips-on-dealing-with-paparazzi.

P. 40, Ward, "Will's Cup of Tea."

P. 41, Morton, *William & Catherine: A Royal Wedding*, p. 131.

P. 41, Morton, *William & Catherine: A Royal Wedding*, p. 128.

P. 43, Nicholl, *William and Harry: Behind the Palace Walls*, p. 248.

P. 43, Ward, Vicky. "Will's Cup of Tea."

P. 43, Nicholl, *William and Harry: Behind the Palace Walls*, p. 193.

P. 44, Nicholl, *William and Harry: Behind the Palace Walls*, p. 249.

P. 45, "Prince William and Kate Middleton Talk About the Moment, the Ring, Children."

P. 45, "Prince William and Kate Middleton Talk About the Moment, the Ring, Children."

Chapter 4

P. 48, "Prince William and Kate Middleton Talk About the Moment, the Ring, Children."

P. 51, Morton, *William & Catherine: A Royal Wedding*, pp. 200–201.

Chapter 5

P. 62, "Prince William and Kate Middleton Talk About the Moment, the Ring, Children."

P. 63, "Prince William and Kate Middleton Talk About the Moment, the Ring, Children."

P. 67, "Prince William and Kate Middleton Talk About the Moment, the Ring, Children."

P. 68, "What We Do," scouts.org.uk/home.

P. 68, Lankston, Charlie, "Inspirational Kate, My Hands-On Scout: Prince Charles Singles Out Daughter-in-Law's Work," www.dailymail.co.uk/news/article-2508593/Prince-Charles-singles-Kate-Middletons-Scout-Association-work.html.

P. 69, English, Rebecca, "Painting the Town Red: Duchess of Cambridge Gets Creative in Art Class as She Visits School in Oxford," www.dailymail.co.uk/femail/article-2104227/Kate-Middleton-Duchess-Cambridge-makes-visit-royal-patron-The-Art-Room-Orla-Kiely-dress.html.

P. 69, Nicholl, Katie, "Meet the Parents," www.vanityfair.com/society/features/2011/04/meet-the-middletons-201104.

P. 70, English, Rebecca, "I'm Thrilled! Kate Puts on a Brave Face as She Sees First Official Portrait Critics Are Calling 'Rotten,'" www.dailymail.co.uk/news/article-2260655/Kate-Middleton-Rotten-official-portrait-Duchess-Cambridge-artist-Paul-Emsley-unveiled.html#ixzz2HfRSVdgZ.

P. 70, English, "I'm Thrilled! Kate Puts on a Brave Face as She Sees First Official Portrait Critics Are Calling 'Rotten.'"

P. 70, "Kate Portrait: First Painting Gets Mixed Reviews," www.bbc.co.uk/news/uk-20978904.

P. 70, English, "I'm Thrilled! Kate Puts on a Brave Face as She Sees First Official Portrait Critics Are Calling 'Rotten.'"

Chapter 6

P. 76, Nicholl, Katie, "Curious About George," www.vanityfair.com/society/2013/10/kate-middleton-post-baby-life.

P. 77, "British Royal Succession Laws to Change," www.
globalpost.com/dispatch/news/regions/europe/unit-
ed-kingdom/111028/british-royal-succession-laws-
changed-prince-william-kate-daughter-queen.

P. 78, "Royal Baby: Kate Gives Birth to Boy," www.bbc.
co.uk/news/uk-23413653.

P. 78, "Royal Baby: Kate Gives Birth to Boy."

P. 79, Nicholl, "Curious About George."

P. 79, Nicholl, "Curious About George."

P. 79, Nicholl, "Curious About George."

P. 79, "Prince William and Kate Name Their Baby
George Alexander Louis," www.people.com/people/
package/article/0,,20395222_20720024,00.html.

P. 80, Nicholl, "Curious About George."

P. 80, Nicholl, "Curious About George."

P. 80, Nicholl, "Curious About George."

P. 81, Nicholl, "Curious About George."

P. 83, Smith-Spark and Foster, "Baby Prince George Is
Christened, 7 Godparents Named."

P. 84, Nicholl, "Curious About George."

GLOSSARY

A-levels Refers to an academic qualification offered by educational institutions throughout Great Britain. To earn an A-level, students must study a certain subject over a two-year period and pass an examination on that subject. Many universities in the United Kingdom use A-levels to determine which students should be admitted.

abdication The act of renouncing a throne.

absolute primogeniture The passage of one's titles, property, and other assets to one's eldest child, regardless of gender. This stands in contrast to male primogeniture, in which titles, property, and other assets are passed to the eldest son.

archipelago A group of islands.

aristocracy A class of society that holds hereditary titles, positions, and land.

British Commonwealth Now called the Commonwealth of Nations, the British Commonwealth consists of fifty-three member states, most of which were at one time territories under the former British Empire. Member states include Canada, Australia, New Zealand, Barbados, Jamaica, India, and more.

coat of arms A heraldic shield, typically representing a person, family, or country.

commoner Someone who is not a member of the aristocracy or nobility.

conjugal coat of arms A coat of arms that represents a married couple. It features both the man's and the woman's coat of arms alongside each other's clan rather than blended into a single shield.

coronation A ceremony in which a sovereign is officially crowned.

cortège A funeral procession.

council house A low-rent home provided by the British government.

courtier Someone who attends to the royal court as a companion or an advisor.

Dissolution of the Monasteries The Dissolution of the Monasteries occurred under Henry VIII, who had severed ties with the Catholic Church in Rome, declaring himself head of the new Church of England.

Domesday Book A book commissioned by William the Conqueror and written in 1086 that contains the results of a great land survey. It listed the land and resources owned in England—some 13,418 places in all—for the purposes of taxation.

Duke of Edinburgh Gold Award The Duke of Edinburgh Gold Award is given to young people who complete a program of activities that includes volunteering, taking part in physical activities, developing life skills, planning and completing an expedition, and working away from home. Students who fail to complete all five of these activities may be eligible for Silver or Bronze awards.

elocution The skill of distinct pronunciation and articulation in speech.

flat Another word for "apartment."

Fourth Estate The press, or journalism.

impaled coat of arms A coat of arms that blends one family's or person's coat of arms with another's, joining them into a single shield.

lady-in-waiting A female member of a royal court who attends to a queen, princess, or other high-ranking noblewoman. A lady-in-waiting is more like a companion than a servant to her mistress.

male primogeniture The passage of one's titles, property, and other assets to one's eldest son.

netball A game that is similar to basketball.

new money Refers to rich people whose wealth has been only recently acquired rather than inherited. Also called *nouveau riche*, new money stands in comparison to old money, or people of a high social class whose wealth is inherited.

Norman Conquest The conquest of England in 1066 by an army of Norman, Breton, and French soldiers, led by Duke William II of Normandy, later referred to as "William the Conqueror."

old money Refers to rich people of a high social class whose wealth is inherited. Stands in comparison to new money, or *nouveau riche*—that is, rich people whose wealth has been only recently acquired.

paparazzi Photographers who follow famous people to take their pictures. They then sell these pictures to newspapers or magazines.

patronage The giving of support, encouragement, privilege, or financial aid to an individual or organization.

prefect A prefect is given the job of helping to watch over and even discipline younger students at a school.

public school In the United Kingdom, a "public school" is what people elsewhere might call a "private school." That is, it's a school that requires students to pay tuition—often quite a large sum—in order to attend.

rounders A game, similar to baseball, that is played with a ball and a bat.

state school What those outside the United Kingdom would call a "public school." A state school is funded and managed by the local government.

succession The inheritance of a title, office, property, etc.

tarmac Like asphalt, a material used for surfacing roads. Tarmac consists of crushed rock mixed with tar.

FURTHER INFORMATION

Books

Andersen, Christopher P. *William and Kate: A Royal Love Story*. New York, NY: Gallery, 2011.

Cywinski, Sarah. *Kate: Style Princess: The Fashion and Beauty Secrets of Britain's Most Glamorous Royal*. London, England: John Blake, 2011.

Joseph, Claudia. *Kate: Kate Middleton: Princess in Waiting*. New York, NY: Avon, 2009.

Moody, Marcia. *Kate: A Biography*. London, England: Michael O'Mara, 2013.

Morton, Andrew. *William & Catherine: A Royal Wedding*. New York, NY: St. Martin's, 2011.

Nicholl, Katie. *Kate: The Future Queen*. New York, NY: Weinstein, 2013.

Nicholl, Katie. *William and Harry: Behind the Palace Walls*. New York, NY: Weinstein, 2010.

Orme, Alisande Healy. *Kate Style: Chic and Classic Look*. London, England: Plexus, 2011.

Articles

Katie Nicholl, "Meet the Parents." *Vanity Fair*, April 2011.

Katie Nicholl, "Mr. and Mrs. Wales," *Vanity Fair*, July 2011.

Katie Nicholl, "Curious About George," *Vanity Fair*, October 2013.

Nicholas Witchell, "Royal Wedding: The Kate Middleton Story," BBC News, November 2010.

Website

The Official Website of the British Monarchy
www.royal.gov.uk
This website is a great resource for information about the royal family. Read historic speeches made by the queen, download royal images, and more.

BIBLIOGRAPHY

"Action on Addiction." Accessed December 17, 2013. www.each.org.uk.

Adams, William L. "Kate Middleton's Secret Confirmation: How Religious Is the Future Princess?" *Time*, April 14, 2011. Accessed December 12, 2013. newsfeed.time.com/2011/04/14/kate-middletons-secret-confirmation-how-religious-is-the-future-princess.

Alleyne, Richard. "Duchess of Cambridge to Be a Scout Leader as Well as Patron of Four Charities." *The Telegraph*, January 5, 2012. Accessed December 17, 2013. www.telegraph.co.uk/news/uknews/theroyalfamily/8992650/Kate-Middleton-to-be-a-Scout-leader-as-well-as-patron-of-four-charities.html.

Andersen, Christopher P. *William and Kate: A Royal Love Story*. New York, NY: Gallery, 2011.

Arsenault, Bridget. "Diamond Jubilee: The Great Flotilla of Queenly Celebration Boasted Kate and Pippa in Red, White, and Blue." *VanityFair.com*, June 4, 2012. Accessed December 17, 2013. www.vanityfair.com/online/daily/2012/06/diamond-jubilee-celebration-london-queen-kate-pippa.

Arsenault, Bridget. "The First Official Prince George Baby Portrait Features Duchess Kate in a Breastfeeding-Friendly Dress." *VanityFair.com*, August 20, 2013. Accessed December 20, 2013. www.vanityfair.com/ online/daily/2013/08/official-prince-george-baby-por- trait-kate-breastfeeding.

Arsenault, Bridget. "Pippa's Legal Team Cites "Serious Distress," Asks for Reprieve From Paparazzi." *VanityFair.com*, January 19, 2012. Accessed December 5, 2013. www.vanityfair.com/online/daily/2012/01/ Pippas-Legal-Team-Cites-Serious-Distress-Asks-for- Reprieve-From-Paparazzi.

Ball, Sarah. "Kate Middleton's Wedding Dress: A Creamy- White, Lace-Sleeved Homage to Grace Kelly." *VanityFair.com*, April 29, 2011. Accessed December 12, 2013. www.vanityfair.com/online/daily/2011/04/ kate-middletons-wedding-dress-a-creamy-white-lace- sleeved-homage-to-grace-kelly.

Ball, Sarah. "Why Is Duchess Kate's Morning-Sickness Hospitalization Expected to Last So Long?" *VanityFair.com*, December 3, 2012. Accessed December 19, 2013. www.vanityfair.com/online/daily/2012/12/ kate-middleton-morning-sickness-hospital.

"British Royal Succession Laws to Change." *GlobalPost*, October 28, 2011. Accessed December 19, 2013. www. globalpost.com/dispatch/news/regions/europe/unit- ed-kingdom/111028/british-royal-succession-laws- changed-prince-william-kate-daughter-queen.

Corneau, Allison, and Omid Scobie. "Kate Middleton: How Prince William's Wife Renovated Kensing- ton Palace." *Us Weekly*, November 4, 2013. Accessed December 20, 2013. www.usmagazine.com/celeb- rity-news/news/kate-middleton-how-prince-williams-wife-renovated-kensington-palace-2013411.

Cywinski, Sarah. *Kate: Style Princess: The Fashion and Beauty Secrets of Britain's Most Glamorous Royal.* London, England: John Blake, 2011.

"Dissolution of the Monasteries." British Library. Accessed December 2, 2013. www.bl.uk/learning/timeline/item106122.html.

"Domesday Book Online, The: Frequently Asked Questions." The Domesday Book Online. Accessed December 3, 2013. www.domesdaybook.co.uk/faqs.html.

Duboff, Josh. "Kate Middleton Reemerges in Breton Stripes, Already Skinnier Than You." *VanityFair.com*, August 27, 2013. Accessed December 20, 2013. www.vanityfair.com/online/daily/2013/08/kate-middleton-reemerges-in-breton-stripes-already-skinnier-than-you.

"Duchess Kate: Kate Loves: Bucklebury." Duchess Kate: Following the Life and Style of the Duchess of Cambridge, August 6, 2013. Accessed December 3, 2013. hrhduchesskate.blogspot.com/2013/08/kate-loves-bucklebury.html.

"The Duchess of Cambridge." Official Website of the British Monarchy, The. Accessed December 3, 2013. www.royal.gov.uk/ThecurrentRoyalFamily/TheDuchessofCambridge/TheDuchessofCambridge.aspx.

"Duchess of Cambridge Due to Give Birth in July." BBC News, January 14, 2013. Accessed December 19, 2013. www.bbc.co.uk/news/uk-21009648.

East Anglia's Children's Hospices. "About Us." Accessed December 17, 2013. www.each.org.uk/about_us.

Eggenberger, Nicole, and Omid Scobie. "Kate Middleton: Inside Her Life as a New Mom to Baby Prince George." *Us Weekly*, November 28, 2013.

English, Rebecca. "I'm Thrilled! Kate Puts on a Brave Face as She Sees First Official Portrait Critics Are Calling "Rotten." *Mail Online*, January 11, 2013. Accessed December 17, 2013. www.dailymail.co.uk/news/article-2260655/Kate-Middleton-Rotten-official-portrait-Duchess-Cambridge-artist-Paul-Emsley-unveiled.html#ixzz2HfRSVdgZ.

English, Rebecca. "Painting the Town Red: Duchess of Cambridge Gets Creative in Art Class as She Visits School in Oxford." *Mail Online*, February 22, 2012. Accessed December 17, 2013. www.dailymail.co.uk/femail/article-2104227/Kate-Middleton-Duchess-Cambridge-makes-visit-royal-patron-The-Art-Room-Orla-Kiely-dress.html.

English, Rebecca. "Wish You Were Heir! Prince William Whisks Kate Away on a £4,000-a-Night Tropical Honeymoon 'in the Seychelles.'" *Mail Online*, May 10, 2011. Accessed December 12, 2013. www.dailymail.co.uk/news/article-1385435/Seychelles-Prince-William-Kate-Middletons-4k-night-royal-honeymoon.html.

"Ex-royal Aide Condemns Paparazzi." BBC News, September 1, 2007. Accessed December 5, 2013. news.bbc.co.uk/2/hi/6245061.stm.

Grill, Theresa. "Introducing the 2012 Style Issue, Starring Cover Ladies Kate Middleton and Jessica Chastain." *VanityFair.com*, July 31, 2012.

Hartley-Parkinson, Richard, and Rebecca English. "Kate Middleton Gets Her Very Own Coat of Arms in Time for Royal Wedding (and Handily It Can Be Used for the Family Business Too)." *Mail Online*, April 19, 2011. Accessed December 12, 2013. www.dailymail.co.uk/news/article-1378441/Royal-Wedding-Kate-Middleton-gets-coat-arms-use-family-business-too.html.

"HRH The Duchess of Cambridge Becomes Royal Patron of The Art Room." The Art Room. Accessed December 17, 2013. www.theartroom.org.uk/7-20120105-patron-announcement.html.

Joseph, Claudia. *Kate: Kate Middleton: Princess in Waiting*. New York, NY: Avon, 2009.

Joseph, Claudia. "Revealed: Secrets of the Middletons' Money and How Kate's Ancestors Made a Fortune." *Mail Online*, March 23, 2009. Accessed December 3, 2013. dailymail.co.uk/femail/article-1163716/Revealed-Secrets-Middletons-money-Kates-ancestors-fortune.html.

"Kate Middleton." *PEOPLE.com*. Accessed December 3, 2013. www.people.com/people/kate_middleton.

"Kate Middleton 'First Laid Eyes on Prince William as a 10-Year-Old Schoolgirl.'" *The Telegraph*, July 27, 2007. Accessed December 3, 2013. www.telegraph.co.uk/news/uknews/royal-wedding/8162448/Kate-Middleton-first-laid-eyes-on-Prince-William-as-a-10-year-old-schoolgirl.html.

"Kate Portrait: First Painting Gets Mixed Reviews." BBC News, November 1, 2013. Accessed December 17, 2013. www.bbc.co.uk/news/uk-20978904.

Knight, Kevin. *Catholic Encyclopedia*, s.v. "Anglicanism." New York, NY: Catholic Online, 2013. Accessed December 12, 2013. www.newadvent.org/cathen/01498a.htm.

Knight, Kevin. *Catholic Encyclopedia*, s.v. "Reading Abbey." New York, NY: Catholic Online, 2013. Accessed December 3, 2013. www.newadvent.org/cathen/12673a.htm.

Lankston, Charlie. "Inspirational Kate, My Hands-On Scout: Prince Charles Singles Out Daughter-in-Law's Work." *Mail Online*, November 16, 2013. Accessed December 17, 2013. www.dailymail.co.uk/news/article-2508593/Prince-Charles-singles-Kate-Middletons-Scout-Association-work.html.

McCorkell, Andrew, and Stephen Bates. "Royal Wedding Date Set for 29 April." *theguardian.com*, November 23, 2010.

Merriam-Webster's Collegiate Dictionary. 11th ed. Springfield, MA: Merriam-Webster, 2003.

"Middleton Coat of Arms, The." The Duke and Duchess of Cambridge. Accessed December 17, 2013.

Moody, Marcia. *Kate: A Biography*. London, England: Michael O'Mara, 2013.

Moody, Marcia. "Secrets of the Royal Romantic Reunion That Changed the Course of History: What Really Made Kate and Wills Rekindle Their Love — and Transform the Monarchy Forever." *Mail Online*, July 6, 2013. Accessed December 3, 2013. www.dailymail.co.uk/femail/article-2357494/What-really-Kate-Middleton-Prince-William-rekindle-love--secrets-romantic-reunion-.html.

Morton, Andrew. *William & Catherine: A Royal Wedding.* New York, NY: St. Martin's, 2011.

Natural History Museum. "Museum Information." Accessed December 17, 2013. www.nhm.ac.uk/about-us/museum-information/index.html.

Nicholl, Katie. "Curious About George." *Vanity Fair,* October 2013. Accessed December 20, 2013. www.vanityfair.com/society/2013/10/kate-middleton-post-baby-life.

Nicholl, Katie. "Kate Middleton's First Boyfriend Finds Love with Girl Who Bears Striking Resemblance to Duchess." *Mail Online,* September 5, 2011. Accessed December 3, 2013. www.dailymail.co.uk/tvshowbiz/article-2033516/Kate-Middletons-boyfriend-finds-love-girl-bears-resemblance-Duchess.html.

Nicholl, Katie. *Kate: The Future Queen.* New York, NY: Weinstein, 2013.

Nicholl, Katie. "Meet the Parents." *Vanity Fair,* April 2011. Accessed December 5, 2013. www.vanityfair.com/society/features/2011/04/meet-the-middletons-201104.

Nicholl, Katie. "Mr. and Mrs. Wales." *Vanity Fair,* July 2011. Accessed December 12, 2013. www.vanityfair.com/society/features/2011/07/prince-william-kate-middleton-201107.

Nicholl, Katie. *William and Harry: Behind the Palace Walls.* New York, NY: Weinstein, 2010.

Orme, Alisande Healy. *Kate Style: Chic and Classic Look.* London, England: Plexus, 2011.

Owen, Pamela. "Ruling the Waves: Three Generations of Royals Join the Queen as She Sets Sail down the Thames on Glorious Jubilee River Pageant." *Mail Online*, June 30, 2012. Accessed December 17, 2013. www.dailymail.co.uk/news/article-2153969/Queens-Diamond-Jubilee-Three-generations-Royals-join-Queen-sets-sail-Thames-glorious-Jubilee-river-pageant.html.

"Palace Advised Kate Middleton to Watch Footage of Diana for Tips on Dealing with Paparazzi." *Vanity Fair*, March 2011. Accessed December 5, 2013. www.vanityfair.com/online/daily/2011/03/palace-advised-kate-middleton-to-watch-footage-of-diana-for-tips-on-dealing-with-paparazzi.

"Party Pieces." Party Pieces. Accessed December 3, 2013. www.partypieces.co.uk.

Peskoe, Ashley. "The Start of Prince William and Kate Middleton's Love Story." ABC News, April 12, 2011. Accessed December 3, 2013. abcnews.go.com/International/Royal_Wedding/kate-middleton-prince-williams-romance-st-andrews/story?id=13356247.

"Prince William and Kate Middleton Talk About the Moment, the Ring, Children." ABC News, November 16, 2010. Accessed December 12, 2013. abcnews.go.com/Entertainment/prince-william-kate-middleton-interview-transcript/story?id=12163826.

"Prince William and Kate Name Their Baby George Alexander Louis." *PEOPLE.com*, July 24, 2013. Accessed December 20, 2013. www.people.com/people/package/article/0,,20395222_20720024,00.html.

"Queen and the Church of England." Official Website of the British Monarchy, The. Accessed December 12, 2103. www.royal.gov.uk/MonarchUK/QueenandChurch/QueenandtheChurchofEngland.aspx.

Rayner, Gordon. "Kate Middleton Family Photos Reveal Her Time in Jordan." *The Telegraph*, March 7, 2011. Accessed December 3, 2013. www.telegraph.co.uk/news/uknews/royal-wedding/8366374/Kate-Middleton-family-photos-reveal-her-time-in-Jordan.html.

"Royal Baby: Kate Gives Birth to Boy." BBC News, July 22, 2013. Accessed December 19, 2013. www.bbc.co.uk/news/uk-23413653.

"Royal Duties." Accessed December 17, 2013. www.dukeandduchessofcambridge.org.

"Royal Involvement with Charities." Official Website of the British Monarchy, The. Accessed December 17, 2013. www.royal.gov.uk/CharitiesandPatronages/Royal%20involvement%20with%20charities/Royal%20involvement%20with%20charities.aspx.

Sacks, Rebecca. "Katie Nicholl: The Secrets of Kate and William's Lovers' Pact." *VanityFair.com*, March 30, 2011. Accessed December 17, 2013. www.vanityfair.com/online/daily/2011/03/-caption-here-weinstein-books.

Sacks, Rebecca. "Royal-Wedding Jewelry: Kate Middleton Wears the Cartier Halo Tiara." *VanitFair.com*, April 29, 2011. Accessed December 12, 2013. www.vanityfair.com/online/daily/2011/04/kate-middletons-tasteful-tiara.

Saul, Heather. "'The Great Kate Wait': Duchess of Cambridge 'Doing Well' in Labour at London's St Mary's Hospital." *The Independent*, July 22, 2013. Accessed December 19, 2013. www.independent.co.uk/news/uk/home-news/the-great-kate-wait-duchess-of-cambridge-doing-well-in-labour-at-londons-st-marys-hospital-8725599.html.

Smith-Spark, Laura, and Max Foster. "Baby Prince George Is Christened, 7 Godparents Named." CNN, January 1, 1970. Accessed December 20, 2013. www.cnn.com/2013/10/23/world/europe/prince-george-christening.

Takeda, Allison, and Omid Scobie. "Prince George Given Four Heifers, Bull, Goat as Christening Gift From Kenyan Tribe." *Us Weekly*, November 29, 2013. Accessed December 20, 2013. www.usmagazine.com/celebrity-news/news/prince-george-given-four-heifers-bull-goat-as-christening-gift-from-kenyan-tribe-20132911.

Thomas-Bailey, Carlene, and Zoe Wood. "How the 'Duchess of Cambridge Effect' Is Helping British Fashion in US." *TheGuardian.com*, March 31, 2012. Accessed December 5, 2013. www.theguardian.com/uk/2012/mar/30/kate-duchess-of-cambridge-fashion-lk-bennett.

Tieck, Sarah. *Kate Middleton: Real-Life Princess*. Edina, MN: ABDO Publishing, 2012.

Townsend, Allie. "Queen Kate? Her Royal Highness? In Search of Kate Middleton's New Title." *Time*, November 16, 2010. Accessed December 17, 2013. newsfeed.time.com/2010/11/16/queen-kate-her-royal-highness-in-search-of-kate-middletons-new-title.

University of St. Andrews. "History of the University."
Accessed December 5, 2013. www.st-andrews.ac.uk/
about/historyoftheuniversity.

Ward, Vicky. "Will's Cup of Tea." *Vanity Fair*, November
2008. Accessed December 5, 2013. www.vanityfair.
com/style/features/2008/11/middleton200811.

Waxman, Olivia B. "'Conjugal Coat of Arms' for Will
and Kate." *Time*, September 27, 2013. Accessed
December 17, 2013. newsfeed.time.com/2013/09/27/
a-conjugal-coat-of-arms-for-will-and-kate.

Westminster Abbey. "History." Accessed December 11,
2013. www.westminster-abbey.org/our-history.

"What We Do." *Place2Be*. Accessed December 17, 2013.
www.place2be.org.uk.

"What We Do." Scouts. Accessed December 17, 2013.
scouts.org.uk/home.

"Windsor Castle." Royal Borough of Windsor and
Maidenhead. Accessed December 3, 2013. www.
windsor.gov.uk/things-to-do/windsor-castle-p43983.

Witchell, Nicholas. "Royal Wedding: The Kate
Middleton Story." BBC News, November 16, 2010.
Accessed December 3, 2013. www.bbc.co.uk/news/
uk-11767308.

INDEX

ABOUT THE AUTHOR

Kate Shoup has authored more than twenty-five books and has edited scores more. The subjects have included computers, crafts, and how-to books, business, and grammar. Kate has also co-written a feature-length screenplay (and starred in the ensuing film) and worked as the sports editor for *NUVO Newsweekly*. When not writing, Kate, an IndyCar fanatic, loves to ski, read, and ride her motorcycle. She lives in Indianapolis with her fiancé, her daughter, and their dog. To learn more about Kate and her work, visit www.kateshoup.com.